Project Management for Authors

FIVE STEPS TO SUCCESS

Fritze Roberts

A Peculiar Project
ERIE, PA

Copyright © 2016 by Fritze Roberts.

All rights reserved. No part of this publication may be reproduced, distributed or transmitted in any form or by any means, including photocopying, recording, or other electronic or mechanical methods, without the prior written permission of the publisher, except in the case of brief quotations embodied in critical reviews and certain other noncommercial uses permitted by copyright law. For permission requests, write to the publisher, addressed "Attention: Permissions Coordinator," at the address below.

A Peculiar Project
PO Box 944
Erie, PA 16512
www.APeculiarProject.com

Book Layout ©2013 BookDesignTemplates.com

Ordering Information:
Quantity sales. Special discounts are available on quantity purchases by corporations, associations, and others. For details, contact the "Special Sales Department" at the address above.

Project Management for Authors/ Fritze Roberts. —1st ed.
ISBN 978-0-9969151-0-6

Dedicated to Todd Main and his Fellowship of the Quill.

Planning is bringing the future into the present so that you can do something about it now.

— ALAN LAKEIN

Contents

About Planning 1
    Project Planning vs. Novel Planning 2
    Planning vs. Pantsing Your Novel 3
    What is Project Management? 4

Defining Done 7
    The SMART Goal 8
    The Triple Constraint 12
    Summary 15

Building Buy-In 17
    Stakeholders 17
    Summary 20

Tracking Progress 21
    Daily and Weekly Goals 22
    Milestones 22
    Project Objective 23
    Summary 23

Getting Back on Track 25

Compare Your Progress to Your Plan 25

Problems and Solutions 26

Summary 29

Celebrating Success 31

Summary 33

About the Writing Life 35

Recommended Reading 37

Index 39

Introduction

About Planning

Writing, for many of us, is a creative and messy process. It is easy to get distracted by the maelstrom of ideas and language, characters and monsters.

I know, project management sounds like the opposite of creativity. My goal with this book is to give you some helpful tools that place just enough order on the chaos for you to finish your stories and enjoy success.

My aim is to give you useful tools for creating publishable work. I am only including the aspects of project management that I think will help you succeed. This book will not prepare you for a certification in project management (PM).

The amount of time spent on planning in a business setting is not necessary for the beginning to average author. Still, some basic PM practices apply. As they say, a little planning goes a long way.

UNDERSTAND:
Place just enough order on the chaos for you to finish your stories and enjoy success.

In this book we'll discuss five steps from project management that will help you get more out of your life as a writer. These practices can help you become more productive. They can also help you enjoy your writing more.

We'll start by defining your projects. What do you want to get done, and how are you going to do it? Then we'll discuss how to get the support you need.

Next, we'll look at how to track your progress while working on your project. I'll give you some methods for keeping yourself engaged and moving forward. We'll also look at what to do when you get off track.

Finally, we discuss the importance of celebrating success. We'll look at thanking those who supported you and rewarding yourself for your hard work.

Project Planning vs. Novel Planning

There are two layers of planning involved in writing a novel. You can plan your project without planning your novel, and vice versa. In this book we are talking about planning your project.

How are the two different? In novel planning, we're talking about character arc, plot structure, worldbuilding, and other aspects of storytelling craft. You're planning the actual story.

In project planning, you're organizing resources and effort. In this book, I argue that there is more to creating a publishable novel than just writing. Creating a book involves brainstorming, planning, writing, revising/editing, and what I call post-production. All of these things have to happen before a book hits the shelves, and they do require a bit of organization.

DEFINITION:

Post-production involves all the steps taken toward publishing a book, after the manuscript is finished. This includes proofreading, copyediting, layout, author bio and photo, and cover design.

By thinking through each of these steps, we get a better understanding of what it will take to create the book we want. This allows us to develop a reasonable timeline, which in turn allows us to set expectations - with ourselves and others. Even if you are a "pantser," I encourage you to do some project planning for larger works.

DEFINITION:

7 stages of a book:

1. Brainstorming
2. Project planning
3. Story planning
4. Writing
5. Editing and revising
6. Post production
7. Marketing

Planning vs. Pantsing Your Novel

There is a great debate in the writing world about whether we should plan stories or write by the seat of our pants (pantsing). Some people feel that planning inhibits creativity, others feel it makes the creative process more productive. I recommend doing what is best for your writing and for the story you are telling.

Most of the novelists I have talked to do some planning. This does not mean that they all outline the entire plot of their story. Many of us start with a vague idea of how we want the story to end, but we don't know how our characters are going to get us there.

But planning is more than outlining. It includes world building and character development. Historical or technical research. It involves brainstorming alternate ways your plot can go, so you can pick the most exciting one.

You can also think in advance about what you want the theme, or take away message, of your novel to be. If you know what your theme is, you can weave it in from the beginning, consciously or subconsciously.

On the other hand, some people feel their best work comes when they free-write on their topic. They allow the story, characters, and setting to reveal themselves in words. These authors feel this keeps their writing fresh, and allows the story to unfold naturally.

Do whatever works best for you.

What is Project Management?

A project is defined as a one-time effort that produces a specific product or service. Project Management (PM) is a formula developed in the business world that is used to complete projects with a high rate of success. PM helps executives set priorities, make action plans, and evaluate work. Their goal is to make sure they aren't wasting time and resources.

Some of the steps that enable businesses to succeed can work for authors as well. PM provides tools that we can use to evaluate a creative idea to see if it is worth working on. It allows us to set boundaries, giving us permission to call something "finished," even when we could keep tweaking indefinitely. It also gives us some tools to keep motivated.

UNDERSTAND:

3 characteristics of a project:

1. **Creation of a unique outcome**
2. **Defined start and end times**
3. **A one-time endeavor**

In contrast to a project, a process is an ongoing activity. In a project, the goal is to create something new. So, by definition, it is something that has never been done before. A process, on the other hand, is a repetitive activity with the goal of maintaining status quo. The following examples will help clarify.

As an author, you want to write your next novel. This is a project. The unique outcome is the new novel. The start time is the moment you start your research, and the end time is the moment the manuscript is finished. Once the book is finished, you will be done - you won't write the same book again.

In contrast, the writing life is a process. Every day (or maybe every Saturday) you get your butt in chair and you write. Some people write at the same time in the same place every day, others use a timer for word sprints, while still others go to the local coffee shop. Those are their processes.

Pay attention to what works best for you to develop your own writing process. A consistent writing practice helps you get more projects done.

In this book, however, we'll focus specifically on managing writing projects.

Step 1

Defining Done

Setting goals and developing plans to reach them is not a skill that comes naturally to most people, but it is one that can be learned.

In Project Management, we begin by defining, in as much detail as possible, what we want to accomplish in the end. By clearly understanding our goal, we can develop a plan that will get us there.

Goals give us a sense of purpose and direction in a world that can often feel overwhelming. Having a detailed plan helps us focus on productive activities, and turn away from irrelevant tasks. This prioritization helps us organize our time and reach success.

It also reduces stress and procrastination. When we are committed to a particular goal, our brain doesn't waste time waffling. Nor do we worry about justifying why we cannot do something else. A good goal keeps us focused.

In this section we'll learn two ways of setting goals. The first is the SMART goal, which helps us set criteria for success. The second is the Triple Constraint, which helps us to prioritize.

Let's take a look at how to set good goals that excite you, and that you can accomplish.

The SMART Goal

SMART is an acronym for five essential characteristics of a good goal: specific, measureable, achievable, relevant, and time-bound.

Especially when we are new to the messy, creative process of fiction writing, it can be difficult to set appropriate goals, but this is a discipline that can be learned. The SMART goal is one tool that can help.

DEFINITION:

The SMART Goal is:

Specific

Measurable

Achievable

Relevant

Time-bound

Let's take a look at each of these criteria.

Specific

When setting goals, the more details you can include, the better. Specificity helps us avoid confusion when working with a team, but it also helps us when we work alone.

By fully envisioning the specific details of our goals, we become more attached to them emotionally, just as readers are more attached to writing that includes specific details about characters and setting.

Additionally, working through the specifics of an idea helps us to identify possible pitfalls as well as milestone achievements to be celebrated.

In this section, I'll use a pulp scifi book to illustrate goal setting because it's a quirky story, but one that is well-executed. I find it inspiring when other authors are uninhibited when developing their peculiar ideas.

So, let's say you are Andre Norton and you've just come up with the idea that leads to *Breed to Come*.

The core concept of this book is to show humanity's effect on our environment through the POV of a sentient cat-humanoid on Earth, centuries after humans have evacuated. (We'll have to discuss the preponderance of humanoid cats in SF another day.) From the concept, the genre is evident - this is speculative fiction.

Often, it is helpful to think about your market before you begin writing. I'm not suggesting you should change what you write in order to chase market trends, but having a general idea of who your readers are can inform your writing. Will you explore your theme subtly or will it be more overt? If you're writing for a younger audience, you may choose shorter words or less grizzly visuals. In this case, Norton seems to be writing for a general science fiction audience.

Measurable

Already, we have a pretty clear idea of what we want to achieve, but can we be more specific?

Yes. If we make our goal quantifiable, then we can measure our success. The easiest way to make writing measurable is by word count.

It's important that you do a bit of research so you can meet the expectations of your editor, and your audience. Today, science fiction novels can be quite long. However, *Breed to Come* is about 75,000 words. We'll use this as the goal, but understand that it may not be appropriate in today's market.

Below are suggested word count ranges for different fiction genres. Keep in mind that subgenres heavily influence this. You might want to do some quick internet research before setting your own goal.

Common Novel Lengths by Genre

Literary & Commercial: 80-110K

Crime: 90-100K

Mystery/Thriller/Suspense: 70-90K

Romance: 40-100K

Fantasy: 90-100K

Paranormal: 75-95K

Horror: 80-100K

Science Fiction: 90-125K

Historical: 100-120K

Other things that can be measured include number of comments on your blog post or article, number of attendees for your readings or lectures, copies sold, average rating on Amazon, agent or editor response time, etc. As you can see, different projects can and should be measured in different ways. Choose the metric that is best for your project.

In our example, let's say our goal is to produce a 75,000 word draft.

Achievable

Andre Norton (pen name of Alice Norton) was one of the most prolific science fiction authors. She wrote novels for more than 70 years and published hundred of titles. For her, writing a relatively short novel is certainly achievable.

For you and me, achievable might depend on the timeline we set. If you are writing your first novel, it may take you a few years. Learning how to write a novel while writing one is no simple task.

On the other hand, some experienced novelists can realistically produce a novel every year or two. In this regard, you will get better at setting goals as you practice, and as you increase your writing stamina throughout your lifetime.

Do your best to set a goal that pushes you to work, but that you will accomplish.

Relevant

The SMART criteria can be applied to any type of goal. Maybe you want to lose weight, or build a garage, or throw an amazing birthday party for your spouse. Those are great goals, but what do they have to do with your writing career?

Similarly, if you have an established career as a regency romance author, *Breed to Come* may not be the best choice for your next book. Yes, some authors cross over, but usually new books have something in common with past titles so they don't lose their audience.

Your answers to the below questions can help you evaluate the relevance of your project:

1. Does the project feel worthwhile? Are you excited about this story?
2. Does this project fit into my workflow? How will I prioritize this compared to other projects?
3. Does this story enhance my oeuvre? Does it help you meet your professional goals?
4. Are you the best person to tell this story? Do you want to take on the issue or theme of this project?
5. How does this story fit in the market? Has it been done before or is it unique?

Time-Bound

A good goal includes a due-date. Setting a deadline provides urgency and helps you to prioritize. If a project has no deadline it is too easy prioritize other tasks.

Set a deadline for your project and calculate how much work per week it would take you to finish on time. Does it seem reasonable? Is it challenging?

Is there some room for error? You want to be able to succeed, even if a small-ish emergency causes you to miss a few days work. Schedule in some sick days. Be a good boss to yourself.

The Triple Constraint

So now we have a really good goal. We want to write a 75,000 word speculative fiction novel about sentient cats on Earth after humans have left, and we want to submit it to our editor in six months. However, we don't quite have a fully defined project yet.

In project management, people often talk about the triple constraint - scope, time, and budget. The goal of PM is to complete a project as defined in the scope statement, on time, and within budget.

1. Defining Scope

A well-defined scope gives us a clear understanding of the project's major boundaries. The scope defines the final product of the project - what will be accomplished and what will exist that didn't exist before.

The boundaries refer to what will and will not be included. For example, if you are writing a novel for self publication, your project would not be complete without a cover. On the other hand, if you intend to query agents and publishing houses with your novel, you will not need a cover design or layout. You may still want to have it edited and copy edited.

On page three we discussed the seven phases of producing a book. You don't have to do all of those phases for every project. You can define your scope to include a long research phase, or to exclude post-production.

Defining your scope helps you to estimate your time and budget. It also helps you focus on the required tasks and avoid distraction.

In our case, our SMART goal does a pretty good job of defining our scope. We intend to write a novel for traditional publication. We will not be responsible for cover art, design, layout, etc.

2. Estimating your Timeline

Let's say you are struck by a new idea for the next Great Novel. What do you do with that idea? How do you turn it into a novel that people will want to read?

There are many books on this topic, so I won't go into all the details. I just want to cover the basics so we can move forward with building a timeline.

As we've discussed before, individual authors may skip some of these, but in general, novel writing is done in four phases:

1. Planning
2. Writing
3. Revising
4. Post-Production

Think about how much planning you will do before you write. By planning, I don't mean strictly outlining.

Most stories require some research, depending on the genre. Many writers work on developing their characters before they begin writing a story. Others, especially in science fiction and fantasy, focus on world building before they begin writing. Some authors like to plan out their plot before they start writing, but some don't.

Think for a few minutes about how you work, and what this idea will require to become a great story. If this is to be your first novel, you may need to take some time to learn the tools of the trade.

No one way is right or wrong. Just be aware of what your story needs and make note of it in your project documents.

Next, estimate how long it will take you to draft this novel. Again, understanding your process is helpful. If you know that you have four hours per day to spend on writing, and you can produce 2,000 words per writing session, it may only take you a month or two to produce your first draft of a 75,000 word story. On the other hand, if you are a weekend warrior with only two hours every Sunday night, it might take you a year or more.

There is nothing wrong with either situation. What is important here is that you be realistic.

Bear in mind, the number of words you *can* write in one day is different from what you *actually* write every day. If you've ever participated in National Novel Writing Month(NaNoWriMo), you should have a pretty good idea of what your best and worst days look like. Estimate your average and use that to calculate how long it will take you to write your manuscript. Remember to account for weekends, vacations, and sick days.

For me, I write zero words on my worst days, and about 2,000 on my best. I know that it is not realistic for me to write 2,000 words every day for an extended period. I try for 500 words per day. That's just the number that works for me.

Third, think about how much time you will need to work on revisions. If you spend a lot of time outlining, maybe you can produce a clean draft that requires few revisions. Or, maybe you produce a fast first draft that requires several re-writes. Account for your process in your timeline.

If you are part of a writing group, the group's procedures may affect your rate of revision depending on how often you meet and how much material you can bring to each session. Be sure to keep this in mind when developing your timeline.

Finally, some projects require post-production. As we discussed earlier, this includes steps that aren't really writing that are still required to produce a quality book - layout, cover art, design, copy editing and so forth. If the scope of your project includes any of these steps, you will need to account for them in your timeline.

3. Estimating a Budget

Think for a moment about any money you might spend on writing. Include notebooks and pens for planning, notes, and maybe the actual writing. If you take your work to a writing group, budget for printer paper and ink/toner.

If your scope includes any post-production, you may need to hire professionals for some of all of those steps. It's important to do some research so that you at least have a rough idea upfront of your expenses.

Some typical costs for self publishing are listed in the chart below:

Budget Item	Amount ($)
Editing/Proofreading	1200
Cover design (original art/photography)	300
Cover design from Fivver.com	40
Layout (BookBaby.com)	300

It might be helpful to picture the final product and work backwards from there. A print book simply costs more than an ebook. Releasing through a traditional publisher will have different expenses compared to self-publishing.

If you are brand new to publishing, the thought of spending money when you aren't sure you'll make any may feel overwhelming. But think about any other hobbyist. A gardener buys plants, seeds, soil amendments, and all sorts of tools. A bicyclist buys a bike, reflective gear, repair parts, and different tools. A golfer needs a set of clubs, a golf bag, proper shoes and attire, and a club membership. You get the point. Our passions are worth spending a little money on.

With creative work, it is important to take into consideration the joy we get from writing and sharing our stories with the world. Think about what you spend on writing and what your passion is worth to you.

Summary

Applying project management principles to our writing helps us make sound decisions for our careers.

In business, failure to meet any of the SMART criteria can result in denial of funding and lack of support for a project from the executives who make such decisions. In our situation, we have to be that decision-maker.

The next time you need to prioritize your projects, try defining each one as a SMARTgoal and then defining the Three Constraints. You'll probably see one stands out above the rest.

EXAMPLE:

SMART Goal and Triple Constraint for *A Breed to Come* by Andre Norton

Specific - a scifi manuscript about sentient cats on post-human Earth

Measurable - 75,000 words

Achievable - yes, based on experience

Relevant - show humanity's effect on environment

Time-bound - deliver to editor in six months

Scope - completed manuscript

Time line - first draft 90 days; completed manuscript in six months

Budget - minimal (typing paper, notebook, pens)

Step 2

Building Buy-In

You may be wondering why I'm writing this chapter on getting support and buy-in for your project. Yes, writing is often solitary work, but the final product - a publishable story - will include other people. If you are working on a short story or article, your team will be different. But if you are working on a novel or other stand-alone work, you will have several types of people involved in realizing the final product.

Stakeholders

In project management, stakeholders are all of the people affected by a project. This section will discuss the people that will be involved in producing your novel.

Friends and Family

If writing is your hobby, done in your spare time, you may want to get buy-in from your friends and family. Especially if you are embarking on a longer work, or participating in a challenge like National Novel Writing Month, you will want to tell the people around you about your project so they understand why you may have less time for them.

Keep in mind - you are not asking for permission. But you do want their support. You will want to communicate to them how excited you are, and how much time you expect to spend on this project. If you have kids or other dependents, you may want to formulate a plan for ensuring they are taken care of for the duration of your project.

Audience/Platform

If you have published something before, your readers will want to know about your next project. Entice them with a projected release date or tidbits of information on your theme or concept. You'll be surprised by the support you get from many of these folks.

Writing Group Partners

Participating in a writing group is a great way to get feedback on your ideas or concepts before you start writing. Often they can advise you on how to approach a particular topic and let you know if your are headed in the right direction. Even if you're not ready to share your work, it's a great idea to participate and learn from the work of others.

DEFINITION:

A writing group is a gathering of writers for the purpose of reading each others' works in progress (WIP) and giving feedback. Sometimes called a critique group.

- o May be specific to one genre or inclusive of all
- o May read aloud or silently
- o May request WIP distributed before meeting
- o Will include people with diverse backgrounds
- o Can be found regionally and on-line

Beta Readers

When you have a draft that you think is the best it can be, give it to beta readers for feedback. This group should include people whose opinion you value. They may be subject matter experts if you write a historical or a technical book. They may be published authors in your genre, or people who are well read in your genre. They may be other writers who have knowledge of the craft.

> ### Definition:
>
> **A beta reader is someone who represents your intended audience. She reads your entire manuscript when you believe it is finished and points out any plot holes, inconsistencies, or confusing passages.**

It is important to let beta readers know that you are working on a new project and you will be asking for their help. If you keep them updated on your progress, they will know when to expect your manuscript. Communicate with them about what you will need and when.

Agents and Publishers

If you have an agreement with an agent or a publishing house, they will expect you to deliver your manuscript on time and within scope. Before you start working on a new project, you need to understand their needs and ensure that the project will be satisfactory to them. They may define you genre and your completion date, so be sure to communicate with them early and often.

Contracted Professionals

Many self-publishers hire professionals to ensure their work meets publishing standards. You may choose to work with any or all of the following: editor, copy-editor, lay-out designer, cover designer, and illustrator. You want to publish a work that you will be proud of, one that will make readers want to purchase your next book. Hiring professionals can help you do that.

Summary

While defining the timeline and scope of your project, it is important to understand the requirements and expectations of each professional. Many of these people have a heavy workload that they schedule well in advance. You don't want to finish your draft, and find that your release date will have to be delayed because you didn't think to schedule time with your editor in advance. Similarly, you don't want to miss a deadline and tarnish your reputation.

Step 3

Tracking Progress

Creating a novel is an arduous process for 99% of writers. Those beautiful novels you've read in a day or a week likely took years to write and publish. This is especially true for new authors.

It is important for writers to document progress. This allows you to go back and analyze your productivity so you can improve estimates for future projects.

Documenting your productivity also helps you find places where you struggle or where things go wrong. Identifying these weaknesses helps you to avoid them in the future.

Furthermore, in real life as in story-telling, we get satisfaction from a sense of progress. It is very easy to get discouraged in the middle of a long project like a novel. You will be encouraged if you can see that you are closer to your goal every day.

Remember:

In real life as in story-telling, we get satisfaction from a sense of progress.

For a project that takes so long, it's important to break the work down into smaller pieces. I find it's helpful to have several layers of subdivision. Progress should be tracked toward daily goals, milestones, and the project objective.

Break your project down into manageable chunks of work to celebrate the small victories. You've probably heard this advice before, but it's worth repeating. It's also not as easy as it sounds. Here are a few tips to help you along the way.

Daily and Weekly Goals

Most successful writers have a daily goal based on either time spent or word count. I'd encourage you to start building this habit, even if you start small.

However, it is possible to reach your goals as a weekend warrior. In this case, you may want to set a weekly goal. If you can write 1500 words per week, you can reach 75,000 words in a year.

Take a moment to acknowledge your success each day that you write. Documenting your word count in a spreadsheet or on a "thermometer" sends a signal of accomplishment to your brain. Other ways to celebrate these small successes may include reporting to a writing buddy, updating a widget on your blog or website, or tweeting your progress using #wordcount or #amwriting or another hashtag that connects you to other writers.

Milestones

Milestones are points in a project at which important tasks are completed. Examples of writers' milestones include:
- o Character worksheets for all MC's are complete
- o Research of culture, religion, and technology is complete
- o Completion of each chapter
- o Reaching the midpoint of the first draft
- o Completing the first draft
- o Completing the synopsis
- o Completing revisions
- o Querying an agent

Milestones can be used to monitor your progress. Each milestone should have a due date that is included in your timeline.

As you can see from the list above, it is common for one milestone to depend on completion of the one before it. If you know you are falling behind, evaluate the impact this will have on subsequent milestones.

Again, each milestone should be celebrated with a small reward. Buy yourself a new book, enjoy a luxurious dessert, or book a massage.

Project Objective

All of the smaller goals we set are stepping stones toward this ultimate objective. If you've regularly checked in, comparing your progress to your plan, then your finished product should closely resemble the original goal you defined in detail before you started.

When you complete your project, be sure to celebrate with others. We'll talk more about this in the last chapter on celebrating success. Before we get to that, let's take a look at what to do if you find yourself getting off-track.

Summary

Break work down into manageable assignments that include weekly goals, mid-term milestones, and major objectives to motivate and track your progress. Put deadlines in your calendar so you are reminded to check in with your plan periodically.

STEP 4

Getting Back on Track

The first step in correcting any problem is acknowledging that an issue exists. If you haven't been doing it regularly, get out your project plan and evaluate your status.

Compare Your Progress to Your Plan

Compare your actual progress to what you expected. Decide how much this variance impacts your goal, and if your priorities have changed.

From there you can decide how to move forward. If you find you are not able to meet your deadlines, you can make changes to the way you work in order to catch up. Or, you can make changes to your plan to accommodate your situation.

It's perfectly normal to make minor adjustments to a timeline or budget, but be very cautious if you contemplate changing your goal altogether. You set the goal you did for good reasons, and you don't want to switch projects out of ease, convenience, or simple avoidance. When faced with the difficulty of writing a novel, it's easy to let our emotions cloud our judgment.

What are some good reasons for changing your project outcome? If a life event interferes with your writing and you don't meet your deadline, your intended project outline may remain the same, but you will have to adjust the timeline. If you're a pantser, your theme may morph, or your main character may change. It's okay, to make changes to your plan, but do so consciously.

Below are three general tips to help you get back on track. We'll look at specific cases next.

Tip 1: Communicate any change in plans, especially deadlines, to the stakeholders who will be affected.

Tip 2: Look for ways that accidents can be helpful. Even if it doesn't help this project, it may be useful for the next. Make a folder of unused drafts, scenes, or characters that you can use later.

If nothing else, you've learned something about your process. I encourage you to keep brief project notes, so that you can refer back to them when developing the next project plan.

Tip 3: Document your progress. As we've discussed before, tracking progress gives you a sense of accomplishment. It also helps you learn from mistakes and make better plans in the future.

Problems and Solutions

Let's take a look at some of the reasons a writer might miss deadlines.

Not writing as fast as expected

This is common for new writers, especially those who are perfectionists. As beginning writers, we need to build our stamina for writing, just as a new runner must train for months to become competitive.

The advice to write every day sounds easy, but it's not, is it? It is so easy to get distracted, to prioritize family or a paying job, or to feel your writing is not up to par and delete half of it.

In this case, it's important to focus on your daily and weekly goals.

If you are not writing every day, or every weekend, evaluate how realistic your goal and timeline are. Is there a habit you can change, or do you have to adjust your plan? If you're procrastinating, figure out how to stop yourself.

If writing isn't honestly your top priority right now, that's okay. But you may need to reevaluate the timeline you set for your project goal. Remember, a good goal is one that is challenging but attainable. In order to set realistic goals, we must be objective about our capabilities.

Being objective about ourselves is difficult. It is not easy to differentiate our wishes from our actual abilities. This takes practice. Don't be ashamed to make adjustments to your timeline. If you track how far off you are, you will learn what type of estimation mistakes you tend to make, and can correct for this the next time you develop a project timeline.

If you persistently fail to meet your goals, then you need to ask yourself how committed you are to your writing. As Hilary Hauck says, are you willing to look back at your life and say "I almost wrote a book"?

Story has morphed

This happens to a lot of writers, whether they are planners or pantsers. A cool twist grabs you and you run off with it. And it feels good, but then you realize you aren't writing the story you thought you would be. It's time to get out your project plan and evaluate.

The big question here is, how different is it? Some smaller questions that may help to evaluate include:

1. Is it a question of scale?

Take a moment to think about your premise. Is it the right size for your genre? You thought you were writing a short story, but now it's a novel. Or vice versa.

It's possible, in this case, that you've misjudged your story idea's "size". Some ideas are big enough to fill a novel, while others are worth a short story.

To create a rich and complex story big enough for a novel, try combining two story ideas. Add a subplot from a different perspective.

If your idea is growing too large, focus on a moment in which one character is forced to make a crucial decision. Write this scene as a short story. Maybe it can be the centerpiece of a longer work later.

2. Has tone or theme changed?

Maybe you've introduced a comical character and he's taken your story in unexpected directions, but your intention was to write a scathing indictment of gender-based oppression in modern capitalism. It may be that this character provides some needed balance to the serious (and possibly negative) tone of the story. Ask yourself how this character can be used to increase the emotional impact of the story.

If the character doesn't fit at all, cut him. But save your work. He may fit perfectly in your next story.

3. Has your plot changed?

Many authors say their plots twist and turn as they write. So first, don't panic.

Take a look at your project objective. Have the changes to your plot significantly changed the project? If your new plot changes your theme completely, or if this plot brings your story into another genre, you may need to stop and reconsider.

If its impact is not that significant, ask yourself if the change makes your story stronger or weaker.

If you've been sucked into a subplot, try to write your way out of it. See if you can tie this subplot into the main plot.

4. Are you writing, but your story is not progressing?

If you are writing every day, but your story does not seem to progress, stop and take a few minutes to evaluate your work.

Each scene must be important for the plot and for the character's development. Make sure you are only writing the important events in your story. Usually, we need to show the big decisions our characters make and how they handle the outcomes from those choices.

One thing that helps me is to have a very rough outline of the key moments in my story. Every day when I sit down to face the blank page, I ask myself where I'm trying to go. For example, I need to get my main character to the point where he leaves the group, and I need to do it in the next 15,000 words. So what has to happen between where I am and that point? Those are the scenes I *have* to write.

If you catch yourself writing about your characters getting up and eating oatmeal, don't be afraid to stop mid-sentence and skip ahead to the meat of the scene.

I have to accept that a lot of the words I write will need to be edited out later. For me, that's just part of writing. If your rough draft is full of fluff - that's ok. You'll edit it out later. Keep writing!

Summary

Periodic check-ins with your plan help you to understand yourself as a writer. As you become aware of your strengths and bad habits, you can improve your skills. You will get better at setting and reaching goals, and you'll enjoy writing more.

If you feel yourself procrastinating, or avoiding writing, do some introspection to see what is holding you back. Once you understand, you can make adjustments.

While I cautioned against changing your goal in the beginning of this chapter, don't force yourself to work on a project you hate. Understand that you didn't value enjoyment enough when you set your goal, and make sure to take this into consideration if you have to start over.

Step 5

Celebrating Success

The ultimate satisfaction for a writer is knowing that others have read and enjoyed your work. The best ways to celebrate a big success, like completing your novel, is to share it with others. You can do this through self publication or by submitting to agents or editors.

Do something to celebrate reaching this stage. You might throw a small party for your friends and fellow writers. Or you might give yourself a few days off so you can de-stress. Just don't take too long away from writing - you don't want to break the good habits that got you here.

Another great way to acknowledge success is to say "thank you," give credit where it's due, and share your excitement with your friends.

REMEMBER:

When celebrating your success, don't take too long away from writing - you don't want to break the good habits that got you to success.

In PM, a project is closed by acknowledging all of the team members. At the end of a project, get out your notes and review the list of stakeholders you identified at the beginning. Take the time to give good on-line reviews of their work or services, and use social media to thank anyone who helped you along the way.

Even if you paid someone for your cover design, for example, take a moment to express gratitude. As an author, you are probably acutely aware that your day job takes time away from your passion for writing. Assume that others feel the same. They work because they have to, just like you, and they'd rather be golfing or writing or knitting. Thank people for spending their valuable time helping you with your project.

Don't forget to thank people who only had a small influence. Maybe someone offered to help, but you didn't want to take their advice. Thank them anyway. Maybe you got two cover designs and chose the better one. Thank both artists. Let them know you appreciate their time. Don't forget family and friends who offered moral support.

In a similar way, be sure to give others credit when it's due. If your story came from a writing prompt, acknowledge the person who created the prompt. If a colleague in a writing group pointed out a plot hole, acknowledge their impact on your story.

REMEMBER:

Thank everyone who spent their valuable time helping you with your project.

Also, feel free to share your success story so that others may be inspired. This is not an invitation to brag - it is an opportunity to share the journey. When your friends and readers see how you accomplished success, they begin to see how they could do it too.

Remember the people you wrote your book for. Don't think of marketing in terms of spamming people. Think in terms of offering them something special, something you made just for them.

Take the time to be appreciative of your readers. If you can, thank people for reviewing your book. If you blog, write a thank you post to your readers. Make them feel like they are a part of your success.

Give away some copies of your book, not because you want a review in return, but because you want the right people to read your work. Generosity begets generosity, but people can sense when you're being disingenuous.

Remember:

We're all looking for things to celebrate in this life. Don't hold back!

All of these ways of celebrating your success should naturally generate some buzz around your work. There is no need to be pushy or to spam people. Remember that as an authors, we are marketing ourselves more than just this one title. Readers want more work from the authors they like. If you make them feel successful and empowered, they will like you and want more. If you make them feel like they're just another royalty check, they won't come back.

This applies to fiction as much as non-fiction. Giving readers the experience they want - a space adventure, a romance, a solved mystery - and then thanking them for reading makes them feel like they are valuable. People like to feel valuable, so take the time to express appreciation.

Finally, an author who participates in on-line communities shows some of her personality without bragging. Maybe she tweets about dining in her hometown, or calls for submissions. Sharing knowledge helps others, but it also makes her more interesting.

All of these activities should create buzz around your work without you having to become a salesperson. Let the quality of your story do the heavy lifting.

Summary

After you finish your book, you will probably want to sell it to a wide audience, but remember marketing doesn't have to be smarmy. It doesn't have to be underhanded or disingenuous. Always be respectful of your readers, and share your enthusiasm naturally.

The message here is - Be Enthusiastically Yourself. The more you share with others, the more opportunity they have to like you. Be honest, show your excitement, and let your friends be happy for you. We're all looking for things to celebrate in this life. Don't hold back!

Conclusion

About the Writing Life

Good planning and working towards goals doesn't come naturally to many of us creative types. Rather, it's an important discipline to practice because it improves the quality of our work. Becoming a great writer doesn't occur over night. It happens through dedicated practice of the craft. Project management gives us some tools that help us set realistic goals.

Setting good goals and tracking your progress will help you make better decisions within your writing and in your life. PM can help you understand your process and keep yourself motivated. It can help you recognize when you get off track and understand how to get back on course. As you continue to think in these terms, you'll get better at focusing on what is important.

By doing a little planning before starting a new project, you will be better at communicating your needs to the people who will help you succeed. Planning also helps us set a reasonable deadline for our projects, which in turn helps us work with others and plan a successful launch of our books.

Finally, when we do finish our books, we will have a list of people to share our success with. Most book sales come through word of mouth recommendations, so remember to be genuine and considerate when celebrating your success.

We have a limited amount of time on this earth. It's up to each of us to make the most of it.

Recommended Reading

Make a Living as a Writer - James Scott Bell

The Self-Publisher's Ultimate Resource Guide: Every Indie Author's Essential Directory- To Help You Prepare, Publish, and Promote Professional Looking Books - Joel Friedlander

Decisive: How to Make Better Choices in Life and Work - Chip Heath and Dan Heath

The Audience Revolution: The Smarter Way to Build a Business, Make a Difference, and Change the World - Danny Iny

Ignore Everybody: and 39 Other Keys to Creativity - Hugh MacLeod

Writing the Breakout Novel Workbook - Donald Maas

Goal Setting: The Ultimate Guide to Achieving Goals That Truly Excite You - Thibaut Meurisse

Business for Authors: How to be an Author Entrepreneur - Joanna Penn

The War of Art: Break Through the Blocks and Win Your Inner Creative Battles - Steven Pressfield

S.M.A.R.T. Goals Made Simple: 10 Steps to Master Your Personal and Career Goals - S. J. Scott

The Practicing Mind: Developing Focus and Discipline in Your Life - Master Any Skill or Challenge by Learning to Love the Process - Thomas M. Sterner

The 90-Day Novel: Unlock the story within - Alan Watt

Index

Achievable, 7, 9
Agents, 17
Budget, 10, 11, 13, 23
Celebrate, 20, 21, 29, 31, 32
Communicate, 15, 17, 24
Creative, 1, 3, 4, 7, 14, 33
   creativity, 1, 3
Feedback, 16, 17
Genre, 7, 8, 12, 16, 17, 25, 26
Goal, 1, 4, 6, 8, 9, 10, 19, 20, 21, 23, 24, 25, 27, 33
Measurable, 7, 8
Milestones, 19, 20, 21
National Novel Writing Month (NaNoWriMo), 12, 15
Organize, 6
Pantser, 3, 23
Planning, 1, 2, 3, 11, 13, 33
Plots, 26
Post-production, 2, 11, 13
Premise, 25
Prioritization, 6
Process, 1, 3, 4, 5, 7, 12, 19, 24, 33
Procrastination, 6
   procrastinating, 24, 27
Progress, 2, 16, 17, 19, 20, 21, 23, 24, 26, 33

Project, 1, 2, 3, 4, 5, 9, 10, 11, 12, 13, 14, 15, 16, 17, 18, 19, 20, 21, 23, 24, 25, 26, 27, 29, 30, 33, 39
Project management, 1, 10, 14, 15
Publishers, 17
Readers
   Audience, 7, 8, 16, 17, 18, 30, 31, 32
Relevant, 7, 9
Scene, 25, 26, 27
Scope, 10, 11, 13, 17, 18
Self publication, 11, 15, 31
SMART goal, 6, 7, 11
Specific, 7
Stakeholders, 15, 24, 29
Success, 1, 2, 4, 6, 8, 20, 21, 29, 30, 31, 33
Support, 2, 14, 15, 16, 30
   buy-in, 15
Theme, 4, 8, 10, 16, 23, 25, 26
Time-Bound, 10
Timeline, 2, 9, 11, 13, 18, 21, 23, 24, 25
Triple Constraint, i, 6, 10
Writing group, 12, 16
   critique group, 16
Writing life, 5, 33

ABOUT THE AUTHOR

Fritze Roberts is an author-entrepreneur with 15 years experience as a program and project manager, specializing in communication of complex ideas and data. She has worked for arts organizations, medical service organizations, medical research projects, and in healthcare IT. Fritze has served as a full-time development writer where she wrote grant applications and reports as well as annual fund collateral, and later as a program manager of six-figure NIH funded grants. In addition, she has written copy for the web with an emphasis on search engine optimization (SEO).

Fritze is also a science fiction and fantasy author with several short stories coming out in 2016 and a novel in the works.

Fritze is available for speaking events aimed at writers and author-entrepreneurs. She can be reached through her website, www.APeculiarProject.com, or Twitter @FritzeRoberts.

www.ingramcontent.com/pod-product-compliance
Lightning Source LLC
Chambersburg PA
CBHW061346040426
42444CB00011B/3112